in embrace

For the Carmel of the
Incarnation Community.
Every good wish
J. Janda

ALSO BY J. JANDA

POETRY

Hanbelachia
Nobody Stop By To See

PLAYS MOUNTED

Animus/Anima
By Children Deceived
Hey, What Are You Kids
Wearin' Them Leaves For
Julian
Olympus 2000
Quetzals
That Sacred Hunger
Voices

STORIES FOR CHILDREN

Appointments with the Little King
Iñigo
The Legend of the Holy Child of Atocha
The Legend of St. Christopher
The Lost Child
The Story of Our Lady of Guadalupe
The Story of Saint Patrick

IN EMBRACE

Poems for Meditation
and Retreat

By J. Janda

Printed in U.S.A.

Cover Portrait: ***Mother of Fairest Love***
courtesy of the artist
William Hart McNichols

Cover Design: Marjory McNichols Wilson

Book Layout: J. Janda

Printed by
PRESS AMERICA
American Fork, UT 84003

Published by
Life in Christ

ISBN 1-892459-03-7

First Printing: 2000

for

William Hart McNichols

Blessings

Blessed be the shy
blessed be the gentle
blessed be the meek
blessed be the mild
blessed be the courteous
blessed be the reverent
blessed be the humble

for their's is the
kingdom of heaven

blessed be the scorned
blessed be the rejected
blessed be the outcast
blessed be the mocked

for all illusions
as nightmares
must pass

but what shall remain
is each soul's light

flashing forth from
the Father of Light
ringed in constellations
of light now and forever

amen

TABLE OF CONTENTS

Creation: Let There Be Light

Dialogues With The Christ Self

The City

The Self

Some Saints

ACKNOWLEDGMENTS

Grateful acknowledgment is hereby made for permission to use the following poetry in this present volume from the various publishers:

"Assumption" appeared in ***THOUGHT*** December, 1976; and ***LAUGHING***, 1976;

"Before Eternity," "Epiphanies," "Genesis III," "Geography," and "God's Mother" appeared in ***SERVICE 1979,*** Paulist Press;

"California Poppies" appeared in ***LAUGHING,*** 1976;

"Christmas Vigil" appeared in ***AMERICA,*** December 20, 1975;

"Covenant" and "Dialogue" appeared in ***CATHOLIC CHARISMATIC,*** December/January 1977;

"Credo" appeared in ***FOLK MASS AND MODERN LITURGY,*** Vol. 4, No. 5, under the title "Some Reflections on Being an Artist";

"Good Friday" appeared in ***THE CARDINAL POETRY QUARTERLY,*** May/June, 1973;

"Inlet" appeared in ***FOLK MASS AND MODERN LITURGY,*** Vol. 3, No. 4;

"Iñigo de Loyola" appeared in ***AMERICA,*** March 15, 1988;

"Joseph" and "Santo Domingo Corn Dance" were printed as bookmarks by St. Joseph Hospital, 1993/94;

"Jesus Speaks I" appeared in ***NEW CATHOLIC WORLD,*** January/February 1976;

"Marie of the Incarnation" and "Thérèse de l'Enfant Jésus" appeared in ***BEHOLD THE WOMEN,*** Dan Paulos Press, 1994;

"Santo Domingo Corn Dance" appeared in ***AMERICA,*** September 15, 1974;

"Tasks" appeared in ***LAUGHING***, 1976;

"Transubstantiation" appeared in ***THE UNIVERSITY NEWS*** of St. Louis University, September 8, 1972;

"Veronica's Cloth" appeared in ***LAUGHING,*** 1977;

"Veni Sancte Spiritus" from "A Doxology in Honor of Catherine of Siena" appeared in *AMERICA*, March 15, 1977.

▪ ▪ ▪

FORWARD

First of all I wish to thank William Hart McNichols, S.J., for his thoughtfulness and encouragement over the years and his suggestions in organizing this collection.

And a thank you to Marjory, his sister, in appreciation for her beautiful cover design.

I would also like to thank Phil Hofstetter of the *Life in Christ* family for his willingness to handle and carry this first edition.

Much gratitude to Tom Hawkes for his computer expertise in seeing this present volume into print.

A very special thanks to Ted and Mary Jo for helping me put this book in your hands.

Finally, a thank you to all publishers who give new poets a voice in their publications.

And lastly, I must certainly thank the following people: Annette for so carefully proofreading this manuscript; Mrs. Agnes Fiedler, (my pen pal for thirty plus years) for her unfailing kindness and support; and Msgr. Robert Servatius, my pastor, for encouraging my avocation as a writer.

J. Janda, 2000

CREATION:

LET THERE BE LIGHT

Let There Be

That squawk
in the pheasant's
throat

was

aeons ago
when He thought matter
in space

(space
in matter
which?)

and whispered
to each atom His plan
a request

to join in dance

alone—together
with multitudes—apart
and part

forming
singular configurations—
a snowflake

repetition
without repetition
never to

be repeated
yet repeated—
kaleidoscopes

crowning
choruses with
consciousness

in that second—
eternity

Before Eternity

Iris open
columbine bloom
violets appear

self disclosures
of
a second
with
personal history

a slow growing
and
unfolding
lost
in the presence

of a moment

Father of the fragile
Father of change
Father of the delicate

help us move in
fleeing dimension

to be dispossessed
is also to possess

it is enough to be

praised be
your delicacy

Genesis III

If it was
a
big bang

then we
are
star dust

and not just
Eden's
earth nor

all the hills
and
streams—fish

all that
flies
and floats

nor only
those
fragrances

from linden
trees
but also

music—of the
spheres
Plato mentioned

and more

we are part
of
all that has

no boundary
or
limit as

Genesis hints
when
saying we

are made in
His
image— so

perhaps will
never
be satisfied

with anything
other than
embracing all

Perhaps

He whose hand
carved
boulders and
chiseled
cliffs to con-
fine
the sea—and
canyons
could with an
enameler's
skill and a clock
maker's
craft—imagine spider
film
(cobwebs a raindrop
tears)
gnat wings

and a columbine's
colors
convolutions
to
say nothing of the
snail's
volutes, convolutes

and place these plots
in
seeds so that
all
could claim
some
hand in the creating

without
em-
barrassment—

not to mention
the
geode's teeth
of amethyst
or
the grace of
a pearl

which perhaps
surprises Him
whose pulse
may be felt
in the sea

Structure

That inner
scaffolding

of things
whether

a grain of
sand

or dew bead

or skeleton
of a leaf

houses Spirit

which can
teach

as lightning

what a life
span

of study
could

not absorb

Vocatio

Flay him
if
you wish

you will
find
his heart

and bones
are
striped

by design
of
his loving

Maker—

the call
to
show stripes

was before
the
birth as the

Christ's

he is named
Zebra
his is the

office to
cheer
confuse and

astonish

Bluegrass

1

Hints of honeysuckle
in the air

a skunk's slow progress
told by the trembling
of tassel grass and
pokeweed

an indigo bunting
feeding on seeding
thistle

both silk—the thistle
white
the bird electric blue

the swell of corn fields

pilings of clouds with
the sun breaking through

as Hans Christian Andersen
said on his deathbed

"Oh God, I could kiss you"

2

This earth has an
age like me

and when our energy
is spent

we shall leave
behind

what helped us
come to see

Love clothed with
the universe

Burning Bush

A blaze of scarlet
leaves

cornstalks hollow and
dry

the smell of upturned
earth—

on a blade of
grass

one water drop
flashed

colors suddenly

as sunlight breaks
through

a clouded sky—the
feeling

that in a flash God
saw

all and clothed
himself in it

Santo Domingo Corn Dance

This earth

this dust
in my hand

what has
it housed

the song
of a bird

the strength
of an oak

the wisdom
of
a holy man

from it too
comes seed

which when
received

calls down
Spirit

to dance
in a costume
of dust

Epiphanies

1

A spider
thread
between
two firs

sunlight
sliding
the curve

a silent
thrush
looking

through
the
screen

2

The junco
with
feathers

ruffled
from
wind on
Lyon
Mountain

speaking
so
eloquently

with only

presence
and a
glance

his neighborhood
is
rock and lichen

and wind

3

And in the
inlet
the bittern

fishes in
clear
water where

red-stemmed
lilies
grow and

green frogs
rest
in warm sun

and translucent
fish
dart out of

moving shadows
seeking
only survival

and light

4

Up Lyon
Mountain

there is
road
side clover

jewelweed
hawkweed

rock, fern
and
a stream

silver
birch
shedding

boulders
and stone

and from
the
top you

can see
Lake
Champlain

the Adirondacks
roads
hills houses
and
trees—that

all are
of
one piece

and that
what
cannot be

seen is all
of
one piece

and that
who
sustains all

has hidden
in
earth dimension

or so the
heart may
perceive

I am Epiphany

Paradox

Our Source in
every
one—every

thing—as the
painter in
the painting

or singer in
the song

or color in
a columbine

or scents of pine
in forests

fleeting visions
none-the-less real
for their quick
passing

Our Creator

Married to matter
wedded to wanting
something always

realizing who he
is through every

thing—things like

solar systems
universes
galaxies

(a columbine)

planets moons
and stars
infinities of
night

(one dandelion)

through wants
and wastes
nights and days

rotations
revolutions
circlings and
spinnings

whirlings
swirlings

(celandine)

dust storms
howling cyclones
and tornadoes
hail sweeps

sleet
blizzards
screeching winds

(yet in)

bird song
trickling
dripping

a baby is
breathing

who is snoring

in tendrils
vines and berries
in roots and shoots

in swamps as smooth
and silken
as rose petals

as well as
fragrances
so cinnamon or
lilac blue
lavender white

scents of snow
glacier breaths

in berries
in berries
and cherries

snowberries
blackberries
blueberries
gooseberries
in apes swinging
and asses braying

in spots and stripes—
in all eyes

eagle's and owl's
in lemming's and
lion's

in hummingbird
and wren

and stretch!
in ostriches

striches
stretches
stitches
stitching
sewing

sewing the oak's
airy cloak
silver green

the calla lily's
seamless gown

these each
seem less

than he and
are less than

he or I or we
is are was were
am be been will be

could be
should be

shall be
will be

is

we are God
realized
in the making

being in
mothers birthing
in babies breathing
in the aged passing

in the seeding
and
in the dying

and mothers—
in the holding
suckle God

DIALOGUES WITH

THE

CHRIST SELF

Geography

If Christ
is
our earth
who
can uproot
us
what wind
could
transplant
us
only heads
of
trees are
storm
tossed hope
lies
in roots

in embrace

Jesus Speaks I

1

You can do
nothing
without me

why do you
keep trying
to do things

alone?

A child is not
supposed to
lift
heavy things
alone

all I ask is
that
you talk to me

tell me why
you are sad

tell me why
you are afraid

tell me why
you are tired

come to me—I
will refresh
you

2

You are so
afraid
so worried

I know you are
good
in your heart

I know you want
to do
what is right

I know all
about you

I watched you
grow in your
mother's womb—

before you
were born
I spoke
your name

I know when
you
stand up—when
you
sit down

nothing is
hidden
from me

come, waste
some
time with me

3

You worry too
much
about my will

at the right
time
I will tell
you

I will speak
to you
in your heart

it will
all
be clear

I will send
the
Holy Spirit

he will tell
you
what to do
and
what to say

4

You get too
discouraged

you forget
you are learning
to walk

of course
you
fall down

give
yourself
time

I am patient
with you

be more patient
with yourself

I have something
very special
in mind for you

something
only
you can do

don't give up

5

I give you
life
I place you on
earth
for a very

special reason

but you won't
find out unless
you ask me what
the reason is

and talking
is so easy

why don't
you do more
with me?

waste some
time
with me

6

Be kind to yourself
take care of yourself

some people walk
their dogs and
buy them presents
and take better
care of them than
their own selves

and be kind
to others

even if they
upset you

remember
I made them
too

and be good
to your mother
and dad

remember
they make mistakes
too
and I love them
as
I love you

7

And why did
I make you?

and why do
I keep you
in life?

because
   I love you
because
   I want you
   to be happy
because
   I want to
   surprise
   you
because
   I want you
   to surprise
   me

8

I make
everything
you see

I make
everything
you hear

I make
everything
you touch
and taste
and smell

to surprise you

9

But if you
don't open
your eyes

and you don't
open your ears

or taste things
or touch things
or smell things

well then
you will never
know me

all that I
do
is to show
my
love for you

10

Honestly

sometimes
you're just
like
a monkey
at the zoo

pick, pick, pick!

all you do
is pick
fleas off

yourself
or others

leave them alone—
you'll always
have fleas

go outside
climb trees
jump
swing on tires
make funny faces

forget about the fleas

Corpus Christi

Poppies
you are for me
Christ

earth fire
tissue aflame

gentle—
I can touch you
Christ

clothed in the
fragile
glory of
a field

a fleeting blaze
nonetheless substantial
nor diminished
with your
quick passing

as all flesh

"take this bread—
eat—
it is my body
which
shall be broken
for you"

from your dying
heart
shake seed
in my earth

root bloom die
Christ poppies

the breaking bud
shows a
red orange cross

Jesus Speaks II

1

Do not be afraid
I have shown you
how to live

I have shown you
how to pray
I have shown you
how to care
for your brothers
and sisters

why do you worry?

didn't I tell you
time and time again
you have a Father
who cares for you

who understands you

he knows all about
you
he even has the hairs
of
your head numbered—

counted

2

I know you don't
mean
to hurt others

I know you hurt
them
I know you are
mean
at times

I know too that
you are sorry
for all of this

it takes time
if you wish
to forgive
if you wish
to ask pardon

and be pardoned—

it will be given
to you
maybe no words
will
be necessary

trust in me
and
trust others

I understand
you
do you understand me

come, waste some
time with me

3

Whether you live
or
whether you die

you
are in my
hands

Oh, I have a
plan for you

if only you
could trust
me
I do so want
you to be
happy

Shalom

Your voice
has blessed
my day

and though
we must pass

the trees
will not
forget

they were
listening

others will
hear your
blessing

in their
voices and

not be
afraid

Covenant

My child

I know
it is
difficult
to love

I know
it is
difficult

to forgive

I know
it is
difficult

to suffer

but look
I am
taking
away
your heart

and in
its
place

I am
putting
my heart

now I will
be
suffering

now I will
be
forgiving

now I will
be loving

in you
my heart is
beating in you

Tasks

A fist
shaken

against

anyone
or
anything

can be
relaxed

and the
rock re-

leased

to make
fire

to cup
water

to bless
the day

The Light

You cannot
change
others, no

but you
can
see them
with
new eyes

Christ eyes

who sees
all
with respect
and
understanding

Assumption

1

Restored
by
fields blue
with
chicory

knee-deep
with
Queen Anne's
lace

and yellow
with
wild snap
dragon
orange hawkweed

crowded
and
abundant
as
mille fleurs

tapestry

childhood
is
medieval

and forgotten
but
for the unicorn

2

The Unicorn

purifying
the
font by

absorbing
the poison

with his horn

so others
might
drink and
live

why must he
be
hunted and
slain

3

Under the
lemon tree

children
and
virgins

waking to
find
his head

in their lap
are
never astonished

but laugh
and
let him go

4

Oh Christ
my
unicorn

to capture
you
is to slay

you—teach
me
to leave

this hunt
and
see your

spattered blood
in
all reality

5

Vermillion
beneath
gold leaf—

the masters
knew
vermillion
beneath
gold leaf
makes
all gold glow

worn paintings
affirm
their belief

Dialogue

The custom of scapegoats
has
perdured, Jesus,
how
can I live with this

I want to blame
others
for what I do

I cannot carry
this burden—

"Leave all" said Jesus
"then
come, follow me"

but Jesus,
they
will think I'm
crazy

"I know" said He

THE CITY

Veronica's Cloth

Madonna of the Subway

I see you
in
the tunnels
of
the city

dedicated
to
begging
and
non-injury

you do not
crush
the bruised reed
nor
quench smoldering
flax

you are the
trust
of the sparrow
and
field lily

neither earth
nor
heart lies scarred
with
your passing

City Morgue

Handmaid of silence
you
have no property
you
do not belong to
this
city nor any
com-
munity nor can
any
thing bind you
in
your celibacy—
where
will you be
buried
I wonder with
your
open hand

Requiescat In Pace

He laughed
and let go

no insurance
nor land deeds
nor back rent
could claim him

he had un-
loosed those
bonds long
ago—not even

an untouched
bottle of
Rosie O'Grady

could tempt
him
as he left us

for Bridget, Patrick
and
the Fiery Child
whose
comet birth marks
those
who draw too near

for life

releasing them
from
all prior claims

For Jesús García

Perplexer of psychiatrists
bane of social engineering

no tax dollar of yours
contributes to education

health or welfare or the
production of weaponry

what vision have you seen?

The Anointed Ones

Called to disgust

their honors are
accolades of abuse
and ridicule

their acknowledgment
a dime or quarter

their burden
to live Truth
in passing

Truth—hidden and dumb
speechless as marrow

at Baptism
branded by
the Trinity

before they were
born—Yahweh pro-
nounced their name

Terminal Ward

1

So many there
waiting

their bodies
beyond

control as
vegetable

life or healing
itself—

one when told
cried

then smiled
and
made plans to
be
with her daughter

2

In March the
woods

are wet—the
trees

showing no
leaves

but a white
flower

the bloodroot
blooms

if you turn back the
blanket

of dead leaves
and

with your index
finger

dig away the
mulch

you can see its
root

a carrot-colored
tuber

which when scratched
with

the fingernail
bleeds

the bloodroot
flower

more than a
chemical

change resurrection—
root

potentials stun the
imagination

Sanguis Pretiosissimum

1

Leaving
the hospital grounds a
rose
splashed vermillion in
my face

I wiped my eyes
in disbelief after

driving a stabbed
Brother
to the emergency
entrance

he kept apologizing for
bleeding
on the seat covers of the
car
and me as I helped him
onto
the stainless steel cart

that night lying in bed
next
to the wall the
image
on the cross looked
down
while a drop of
blood
from the nailed foot
fell
on my eyes though

I could not move a
hand to wipe away

what
I would
drink
at Mass in the
morning

2

It is everywhere
seeping
out under doors
trickling
down steps onto
concrete
pavements and
into gutters
in Dutch Flemish
paintings
it squirts out of the
wounds
of the Crucified

sometimes angels
are depicted
catching it in
golden cups

Transubstantiation

The flow of blood

out of the chalice
down the white linen
flowing down the altar steps
flooding the chapel floor

shoes darkened
and the red warmth
seeped up trousers
and stockings

the spring
in the chalice
could not be
stopped up

though he had
set the fallen chalice
upright—

God had given
the power
to choose to change
matter
into the body of
Christ

and forced his
hand to cover the cup
till he felt the rim
cutting into his palm

the spring
in the chalice could not
be stopped up

and the flow of
blood was warming
to the waist

a sickening odor
a mad man's vision

blood—hair and
skin stuck to the
rock Cain dropped
by the way

till Hiroshima's
transubstantiation

God had given
the power
to choose to change
matter
into nothing

no thing—no

THE SELF

Reconciliation

The child I
was
is crying in
my
lap and I
am
embracing him

I am father
now
of him and
will
not laugh
when
he tells me
he
is afraid
of
his wishes
and
his dreams

the child I
was
is crying in
my
lap and I
am
embracing him

Paroxysm

1

Milkweed
silk weed

you spit
and cough

angel hair

(I have seen
it on trees)

even in death
you promise

juice and
blossoms
to cover

nude earth
wasted
earth

with scent
and bloom

as poems and
pictures crowd

absurd life
or
so it seems

during reason's
winter until

reason's death

2

Reason's throes

it will not let
go it fears frost

and cold but
it
as all earth

needs seed

which
will descend
on wing

making an
abundance

in want
in waste

3

Angel's seeds
with
angel hair

sing
serviam
and

holy—holy—holy

Patterns

1

Again I was running
from you, Lord

when I fell
into
that field
of
clover filled
with
filigree butterflies
and
enamelled bugs
on
apple leaves

blue chicory
and
running rabbits
and
daisies gold
and
white—all in
full
sunlight

2

I joined Magdalen
in
that day's tapestry
kissing
the foot of your
cross

and later in
woods
wet with fern
and
red raspberry
acorns
and nightshade
I asked if

better or worse
richer or poorer
sickness or health

could make
meaning
when I walked
into
a branch heavy
from
the night's rain
and
felt the cold
shower

and could have
sworn
I heard laughter

3

Was it you
or
those who

weave tapestries
once
they have a pattern?

Knee-Deep in Lake Chateaugay

1

Caught in a
moving web

a running net
of light

which did not
catch the

feet or trip
so some

subtle water web
seemed at

work vanishing
without light

2

Christ touching
through images

so fleeting—
absences

realer than
realities

nightmares—

eyes adjusted
to
darkness

are blinded
by
light

and so close—
some
spit and mud

are required
for
healing

We

I cannot leap
jump
from or out of
this
body flesh bone
house

and now I
am
the only

configuration

I can come
to
feel or know

so

let me love
this
space place

I now in-
habit
before my
breath

becomes wind
and
all for nothing

seduces me
into
lying, denying

my who
that
I am afraid
of or
care for

The Complaint

White pebble
in my hand

you are fiercely
impenetrable

will it always be
a matter of surface
with you and me—

I am learning
to live with you

but your language
is beyond me

beyond my thinking's
noisy machinery

beyond memory's frontier
off imagination's edge—

I have been promised
another white stone

bearing a new name
known only to me

will it too
be impenetrable

I am beginning
to live with you

I am beginning
to see

California Poppies

God is
the
self's

structure

nothing
can
be taken

away

emptiness
is
fullness

the proof
is
the deed
color
form
fragrance

hidden
in
seed

blessing
the
desert

flowering

peace

Good Friday

On old trees
lichen
    green
    and
    yellow
show

on fallen trees
mushrooms
    flared orange
    with white lips
sprout

and near
rotting stumps
out of
curled oak leaves

    spring beauties
    white with
    pink veins
    no enameler
    could copy

open to rain and snow

in a nest
eggs
    smooth
    stones
    speckled
will sing
    of all that is
soon

Spring

1

Rust and dried
blood
mark the petals
of
the dogwood

a legend tells

for the Crucified
had
promised the tree
on
which He was fixed

a memento
for
its wood

a forgiveness
while
his blood was
spilling

2

Layers of white
bloom
in cold woods
before
trees leaf

each
bearing the
print
of nails

even before the seed

they seem like
stars
suspended or thin
clouds
unattached

or touches of
white
on a canvas of
quiet
earth colors

3

And that ache
that
pain— infection

once
lanced with the
spear
from Christ's
side

opens eyes heart
mind
to all life

so much the
dearer
marked by the
blood

to be grasped
and
clung to for the

sake of the Lamb

Easter

1

Rain
dripping down
through
vents in the
empty
subway station

into

puddles between
tracks
with bottles toilet
tissue
cans—cellophane

train to Jersey

then woods—
tangles of thorn
tearing
at the pants and
vines
catching shoes

marsh earth
from
melting snow
under
wax ivy
leaves rotting

though

in a clearing—
snowdrops

up out of
leaf mold
twigs loam

appear
more and more—
they had
been there

2

Memories
of
Emmaus

cold black
earth
breathing its

best life
delicate
white
Christ
prevailing

is/now

after
ashes

Wednesday

because
of an
Easter
morning

"Didn't you know"
he had asked

Pentecost

The sea

surging
swelling
curling

the crash

foam running
advancing on
pebbles and
sand

honeysuckle
clover
and rose scenting
the
sound and

our salt
blood
surging

the swell
from
a source

not seen

we are blind
men
walking a
shore

learning
immensity

following
a beach

Lazarus

How he died
he could not
remember

or why he
died he could
not tell

or whether he
had chosen
death or just
fell into
accepting it
he could not say

he only knew
that a darkness
filled his eyes
which closed
them to light

preferring the
silence of tombs
and the bindings
of cotton bands

till the voice
of his friend
called to him
again—to life

out of the darkness
of certitude
back to the
colors of mystery

SOME SAINTS

Inlet

The sea

in storm
in calm

remains

in cyclone
and doldrums

the sea

containing
supporting

embracing
and
holding

life

in dark
and
light

so the
mystics
say

we swim
in
Deity

Christmas Vigil

A stranger
was
sleeping his
head
in his chest
during

the Mass

I would not
wake
him to share

Christ's peace

nor would the
saints
this morning

nor would tiny
eighty
year old Angela

as she moved
softly past him
sleeping in the
warm church

Angela

who always leaves
her
pew to touch other
hands
as gently as a
snowflake

would not touch
this sleeping man
child this morning

Joseph

Who
loved as his own
what
was not his
nor
could ever be his
but
whom he protected
and
watched grow so
contradiction
could
bloom in mystery
and
scatter blood seed
to
root in despair

and blossom white
as
his staff of lilies

Saint Francis of Assisi

Lord of the Revels

1

So tired
so very tired

how strange
in youth
to endure the

crowning
the continual
crowning
with roses

and yet feel
so very alone
surrounded

is it the delight
of being used
that once seemed
everything

but now is the
cup—empty

the feeling persists
as the ring
returned to the giver
is still felt
on the finger

2

"Bernardone

the trees are
your green
friends

they will not
use you

and the birds
will no more

trouble your mind
than a canary
on your little
finger

the fish
will show you
how to swim
in God

and the ocean
will teach you all you
need know
of theology"

the beggar woman
whispered
before they laughed
her away

"Lady Poverty"

in mockery
they called her

3

It is the time
when

the heart
is troubled
is divided

and afraid
to believe
in dreams

it is a
winter

the death
of the
seed

but the
beginning of
spring

The Cradle of Greccio

We live in God
as in a house

with a roof of stars
and a bed of grass

and we—every
thing
are his dreams

but for our lust to
conjure horror—

though who has looked
upon helplessness

has looked upon God
imaged best in a baby

Il Povarello

"Sister tree" he said
"speak to me of God"

and the almond tree
blossomed

once a wolf
gave up thoughts of
fresh rabbit

even sparrows came
to rest and listen

a saint bringing out
the best—always

what seems against
nature—that hidden

self secret in pith
that gift in marrow

Stigmata

Being loved
by God
and man was

his heart's
assumption

until the
markings

making him
beyond
any doubt

Christ's
undeniable
lover

Christ

the christ
their minds

not Mary's
body had
fashioned

and so they
withdrew
toleration
of him

afraid to
believe
that to be
printed
with pain

may be the mark
of a true lover

The Markings

Wounded hands
may bless
and heal

but no longer
build or
keep

only embrace
to release

while singing the
seraphs' song

in acknowledgment
of the holy—

for the gift
of faith
is to release

with pain
for
reminder

should the
heart forget
while asleep—

each is God's house
his temple
his holy of holies

Our Brother

Yes, Francis
the fool

had chosen
to listen to
his heart

(or did he
choose)

so swelled the
music there

he could not
hear his
condemning
mind nor

the minds
of others
condemning—

he would walk
miles

to his friend's
house for

a cookie

for he could
be kind
to Brother Ass

his body

as well as
the birds

who clothed
him with
their song

and feathers—

and when Francis
spent the night
with Clare

even the house
could not contain
the aura

Elizabeth of Hungary

She was known
for
mismanagement
and
giving away

food and clothes

to the poor
who
bloomed as

extravagantly
as
meadow flowers

both of which
sustained
her but Louis

needed roses
red
and white
to
confirm whom
his wife found

Christ

suffering
and
reigning
and
hiding in all

Three Poems After Julian of Norwich

Sitio

That terrible
thirst
of the Crucified

whose posture
imputed
blame to none

but only
love
longing unto
the
spilling of
blood

so precious
are
we to him
his only crown
treasure
all—he gives

his selfbread
to
become us

and begs only
belief
that forgiveness

is his hunger
us
to hallow

The Comforter

Drink my blood
wine
and know I
would
die a thousand
deaths
for you for
given
unto you is my
promise
sealed in blood

I shall not
leave
you orphans

my Spirit is
given
you—he will
tell
you what to
do and say—for my
Father's will is
that
none be lost

God's Mother

As the closing
of crocus
in early evening

so is his mother's
life hid—
only questions

have we of her
and a
song of praise

and deeds as
petals falling—

as for the memory
the blood running

did she know

past her imagining
were the
deaths he'd suffer

to the uprise of
Easter to
make us laugh

full mightily with
the burst
of birdsong and

the leap of squirrels
to join
in his ever springing

Mother Teresa of Calcutta

1

"At Mass
Christ
is hidden

in bread

on the
street

He hides
in the
neighbor

helpless
alone
afraid

He is all
around us

we must
attend Him"
she says

2

At the
hospital

of the
dying
she shows
that
although

they have
lived
as animals

they must
die
as angels

her
living
hope

to do
something
beautiful
for God

Ignatius of Loyola

Iñigo de Loyola

1

He gave up
thoughts
of suicide

to be of
help
to souls

after a
cannonball
shattering
his knee
taught him
something
of the world

and legends
read
during recovery
pierced
those places
where
sinew joins
bone

finding
God
in agony

first but then
in
stars by night
and
later at day
in
a blade of grass

an orange leaf

he began his
mornings with

"What shall we
do
for God today?"

letting the Spirit
blow
through his soul
as
wind through
a
field of poppies

2

The Spirit

leading
him first

to the sick
prostitutes
children

those in whom
the
newborn Child
is
most found

dumb, helpless

doomed to die
without holy

love which
only
absorbs fire
and
ice to answer

as earth in
April
with flowers

and later
to all who

seek in suffering

the Father
in the Spirit
with Christ—
he began the
Compañia de Jesús

knowing wood
when
cut will grow

green again and
sprout

wood hath hope

Ignatius Collapsing at the Altar

That Jesus could
love everyone

even false lovers
and eat

with them in peace
and mercy

and create of them
a family

whose body he
was—and

teach them reverence
without fear—

caused his body
to first shake

and then collapse
at the altar

grasping the
white linen

and pulling candles
chalice

paten hosts and
flowers

upon himself
to wake to find

Christ's blood
had soaked through

the gold brocade
the white alb

staining his stomach
purple red

The Remembrance

1

"Be still, be silent
I understand you"
he said

while cupping a flower

so a brother witnessed
then told a writer

who perhaps also felt
words as a flower

can hold a soul

2

The word

has a way of living on
in spite of our
uttering it

or do we

be still, be silent
I understand you

Robert Southwell

"That Sacred Blood is still warm,
those wounds still open,
and those bruises may still be seen,
with which God redeemed the souls
that we are tending. At such sight
dangers may well be scorned,
lest such precious pearls be lost."
—Robert Southwell

Neither the pearl
nor the diamond

is diminished
by day or night

nor graced through
ownership

nor changed by price

purity is its
birthright

which craft
cannot create

only cherish
or destroy

Marie of the Incarnation

"Divine love is an inexorable censor:
its lamps are fire and flames.
It wishes to purify the soul yet further,
for there yet remains in the will's power of loving
a trace of self-will to be purified.
Divine love consumes it,
and herein is the sacrifice of the victim,
here finally is true substantial poverty of spirit."
—Marie of the Incarnation

Mist

mosses between
tree roots

green acorns

wet leaves
underfoot

rotting
fallen
trees

rain tapping
maple leaves
in thin layers
above

a rock
cushioned
with moss
she sat here
and gathered
the damp shawl
to herself

the force
the fire
to burn brambles
melt ice floes
even
split rocks

the Holy Spirit

felt before
the news of

Brebeuf
Daniel
Lalemant
so delicate

and the
Algonquin

how many

all dead

close by

an odor of
black earth
where
an oak
lay
uprooted

its roots
still locked around
the rock
clung to
in Canada's
soil

a squirrel
was burrowing
the oil
the lard
the butter

brandy for
domestics
from France
and fish

all lost

the convent had
smoldered
three weeks after
the fire

the novice
had tried to keep
the leaven
from freezing by
placing
a pan of coals
in the
pine kneading trough

and the new pine
spat with fire

the sisters
and boarders
barefoot
watching in
the snow

the last glow

the gutted beams
burnt out

rain tapping
maple leaves

fern and
mushroom

split rocks
wet and black

she gathered
the damp shawl
to herself

glowing axe
necklaces
they were made
to wear

their tongues
pierced
their flesh
cut and eaten
their blood
drunk

Lalemant's head
cleft by a hatchet
his brain seen

Daniel
with
musket shot
and
arrows was
consumed
in fire with
his church

rain tapping
maple leaves
split rocks
wet and black

red berries
on a stalk
scarlet beads

she lifted the
fallen plant

its leaves were
slime
from the wet
but
the scarlet beads
were
tight on the stalk

she did not
know
the name

like
the Algonkin
Montagnais
Huron

she
had come
to Canada
for

scarlet beads
Jogues' fingertips
Christ's blood

for this
she had come
to them

Christ's blood

bathing us
immersing us
flooding us
Christ's blood

must not be
shed
in vain

once
from a canoe
she
had noticed
pale blue and white
flowers
growing
with grass
in a rotted log
on the lake shore

water willow

smaller
than
violets

and she knew

For Dorothy Day—The Water Strider

To whom would
they go

she wondered
then questioned

herself

and yet she
would not

condemn pope
bishop nor priest

for they also
are the Christ
though they
do not carry

shopping bags
nor sleep on
park benches—

◊ ◊ ◊

"Do what you
would wish
them to do
unto you"

a voice whispered
and she responded
with hospitality

with soup and
benches

and bags of
clothing

yes—clothing
and feeding
and housing

the homeless
the rejected
the unwanted

the absurd Christs

who fit not
in churches
nor prisons
nor hospitals

the absurd Christs
who slip through

every mental grid
and
rational sieve

those to whom
no law or structure
can apply

the Christs walking
on water

instead of using
boats or bridges

the Christs reaching
their purpose to live
to love

and embracing it

Anonymous Saint

Snow was blinding
and blowing from
a fierce wind
almost obliterating

one of his dogs
curled up on
his sleeping bag

in the basket of
his grocery cart
next to the storefront

and the snow kept
blowing while

another dog was slowly
wagging its tail
and looking up at
him explaining to
the social worker,

"Ain't no shelter that
allows dogs and I
can't part with them

don't worry lady
they plus the sleeping bag
keep me warm enough

I got all I need—sure
is cold today, ain't it!"

ER: Diagnostic Imaging

The x-ray films
showed numerous needles—
sewing needles embedded
beneath the skin—
lodged in the soft tissue
of the upper torso
and genital area

"Doc," he said seeing
me viewing them
"them are needles—

I used to hate myself
pretty much but I ain't
done that no more

since I seen the Light"

during the exam
I noticed tattoos
covering his body

on the upper
right quadrant of his
back was tattooed

Jesus is Lord

Thérèse de l'Enfant Jésus

Clip the bird's
wing

the desire to
fly

remains like
seeking

the Christ when
the

only meaning is

memory—of a
promise

made while
holding

an opening rose
white

as the wafer
received

believing senses
are
deceived

and that coughing
blood

means only that
the

soul will be
separated
from the body

and the only
position

possible is of
childhood

looking up

The Magdalen

What Magdalen
mis-
placed was

found with
the
breaking of

a pot of nard
and
the innocence

known was
as
spring with

the sun un-
locking
ice lakes

rivers—all
snow
melting losing

old structures
causing
dry seed to

warp and crack
re-
leasing color

and perfume—

innocence

that gift
of
water

acknowledged
in drought

with
temptations
to
close the pores
of
the roots

against
deeper
springs

to choose
not
to thirst

in the
withering

to lock the
pores
of the leaves

against rain

The Temptations of Saint Anthony

1

Who pass through
this
land clinging
to Christ's hand

will learn
that
strawberries are
not
large as man

and though skies
are
filled with imps
as
clouds of gnats

they may not touch
us
only menace
and
confuse for a time

that we may
understand

man He prefers to
Himself

though the father
of
lies would have
us
believe otherwise
and
not to know his
only
power is what
we
give to him

2

For the Christ
did
not consider
His
divinity something
to
be clung to

but left His
land
to be our servant

outstretched arms
were
His only posture

as an infant
to
His death on a
cross

for such the
Father
desired in the
Spirit

3

The Spirit

our flesh
His
dwelling

the Truth
against
which the

power of hell
cannot prevail

The Flight into Egypt

1

To leave all
that
is known

mother and father
friends
the synagogue

home

the tools with
which
one creates

means of survival

for the sake
of
the Child

because an
angel
in a dream

gave warning

2

How could
Joseph
who was nurtured

on cedar odors
the
ring of hammers
hitting
iron nails

who felt the
grain
of wood and
the
bite of the
saw
against wood

fashion a journey
which
had neither
the
sound nor feel
of
what he had known

3

Did the Child's
cry
stop the dream

and wake him
to
the darkness

of the room?

the Child was
crying
but the dream could
not
be confirmed

4

The dream

lived out
in
darkness

following
uncertain
roads

wondering
with
each step
if
oneself is
one's
own fool

to journey
in directions
angels
indicated

or did they?

to Egypts

of deserts
of ciphers
of moons

5

Who follow
them
can explain
to
none yet

some must
follow
for the Child's
sake

because of
angel
voices heard
only
in dreams

in darkness
in sleep
in rooms

Shadrach, Mesach, and Abednego

Fire must be
preferred
to the lie

was their
conclusion

for to deny
Yahweh
was as possible

as denying
the
furnace into

which they
were
cast and

after they
had
sung among

the flames
they
were released

they spoke of
winds cool

and fragrant
as
when the

new grass is
wet
with dew

for they were
no
more harmed

by the flames
than
mountains in

mist or birds
perching
in flowering

almond trees
though
they could

not know this
before
the fire or

that those who
caused
it would be

consumed by
that
which they

would have
them
consumed

Noah

Noah left
his
fear in the

ark with
only
a rainbow

for surety

something
he
could not

pocket
or
cling to

only witness
after
storms—but

that was
enough
to him and

all who
keep
promise

A Doxology in Honor of Catherine of Siena

Pater Noster

1

A passion
to
set teeth
on
edge that

hunger
to
embrace

caused
what stands
create

2

His bloody
death
a reminder

a voice
without words
the proof

and changes
of
season
to
underline

what is easier
denied
than endured

3

He has muted
His
heartbeat

dispersed it
in
bird and wood

marrow of stone

the sun's secret
colors
reflected in rainbows
and
all that it warms

O Bone Jesu

The mystical ring
His
circumcised flesh

gave her

the doubted virgin
to
cry the question

can blood and
flesh
believe His love

ah, the mind can, but
crucifixion requires

an heart's soil—
wood
crosses cannot
be planted nor
stand
in ideas nor can

conceptual lands
support a
body nailed to
a cross
nor can hot blood

spurting be tolerated
in
aseptic atmospheres
where
smells and writhing
disgust—

that she feared
was
the infection

which no scalpel
could
lance or remove

Veni Sancte Spiritus

1

She passed
the
executioner

and kneeling
held
the head of

him bending
over
the block

the blade
cut
bone, flesh

cartilage
her
white habit

was stained
red
but still she

held his head
"Mio
fratello

dolce" she said

2

She had heard
a
voice of fire

and listened
"Cry
Abba, Father"

it said and

"Comfort
my people
comfort them"

3

And so she
lived
until the

forge could
no
longer hold

the fire—
that
fire—no

cosmos could
contain
only trace

or mirror

The Silence of St. Thomas

Did

a shower of
lemon
yellow leaves
against
cerulean blue

cause it? or

those tapestries of
vermillion
and umber leaves
we tread
in autumn with silver
squirrels

or

the sight of his
horse's
oat bucket brimming
with
pigeons—on his
last
journey to Lyons

or did

he come to
rest
in silence

as the trees
after
giving away
all
their leaves

realizing the
desire
to give is the
substance
of gold—the

structure
of
our Maker

that fall day?

All Saints' Day

The presence
of
Trinity
in
souls and

leaves

will always
be
an inner

benediction
at times
of peace

transmuting
the house to

blood
to
fire
to gold
in
throes

no soul
can
claim nor
own

the color

of its new
substance

nor would
it wish to

All Souls' Day

The girth
of
a sycamore

beyond
embrace

like
leaves
re-

leasing
the
tree to

be lifted
up
in dance

higher
and
higher

by wind

un-
seen
as
spoken

words

yet
confirming
belief

so must
be
the exodus
from
purgatory

which we
make
here or

hell also

Christ Our Earth

1

We are given
moments
of clarity

which give
meaning
to what we do

without
obliterating
the fact
of suffering

which we have
experienced
and know we can
experience

a peace
a joy
a knowing

that
what was begun
in us
will be completed
in us

a desire
a wisdom
a love

in us
over which we
have
no control

but much
control

for this
we thank you
Father

2

In our deepest
selves
if we can enter
there

we may discover
a peace
and a goodness

a forgiveness
a gentleness
and a hope

Christ

in our deepest
selves
we may discover
a desire

a most inner
desire
that what we want
is
to do God's will

and that this desire
is all
we can really
know
or be sure of
about
our selves

yet it is enough
it is a grace

3

We may learn that
we are
rooted in Christ

that regardless
the atmosphere

regardless our
stunted growth

regardless our
daily dyings

we have the
potential

we are the
potential

to bloom

because of
Christ
our earth

because of
Christ
our atmosphere

we are the seed
from
the Father's hand
we are
the breaking shell
sending
down roots reaching
our shoots
up stretching toward
our Maker

4

To be rooted in
earth
is to be rooted in
Christ

and to embrace the
earth
is to embrace
Christ

to die
means to lose faith
or
to adopt an old faith

the belief in nothing

  to believe that
  I am nothing

  to believe that
  earth is nothing

to believe that
others are nothing

to believe that
my human endeavor
is nothing

and this is the
mystery of death

that one can die

rooted watered and
warmed by the sun

and say
all is nothing
yet live

5

That old faith
a deceit
a lie
Lucifer's negation
of all that

is created by
the Father

through the Son
in the Spirit

is death

Lucifer's denial that
Christ
could become earth
live
in earth on earth

choose a point
a place
in time
in the universe

which He had made

and be obedient to
it
while following His
Father
in the Spirit

denying nothing
that is—
embracing all

teaching us that to
believe
is to deny nothing
that is—
to embrace all

Lucifer's denial
is death

6

Not to know
or
to forget that

my deepest desire
is
to do God's will

that I am
rooted
in Christ

is blindness—

to deny that my deepest
desire
is to do God's will

to deny that I
am
rooted in Christ

is a lie—
delusion

is darkness
is belief in nothing
is death

He came that
we
might have life

and have it
more
abundantly

7

As plants become
the earth
are fed by earth

we rooted in
Christ
become Christ

to deny this
is
to deny Truth

to abort
ourselves
from Truth

and the
consequence
is death

and here lies the
mystery
of the deference
the respect

of our Father

He will not
coerce
or force our
love—

and here lies the
mystery
of our selves

that having seen
light
we choose darkness

having lived in
Truth
we prefer the lie

8

As fish live
only
in water

we live
only
in Christ

this is Truth

anything
less
is delusion

yet the lie
is
made Truth

and Truth
is
made the lie

9

Yet He will not
force
our allegiance

the struggle
the years
the deaths

for Truth

the suffering
the humiliation
the unknowing

for Truth

can it be
otherwise?

The vision of
the child
the poet
the prophet

Christ

the hope
the dream

the gift
given

the Truth
must
be cherished

protected
nourished

it is a living
thing—
it is a delicate
thing

the fleeting
vision
cannot be denied

a bluebell
blooms
and dies

it was
not
a lie

the flame in
the
sanctuary lamp

must
not be put out

Truth
witnesses
Presence

not seen

10

For what
is not seen
is what we
worship

the Truth
or
the lie

for this
we die

and the choice

is the price
of a life

the cost of
a self

11

And if we
seek the light
we will find

darkness

and if we
seek the spring
we find

the desert

and if we
seek the truth
we find

the lie

His memory a
pinpoint
of light in
dark tunnels

His life
a damp night
chill

His words dry
seeds
lying on rock

but if we
break
our earth
and
bury His seed
and
water it
and
wait and
watch

His seed in us
will
grow—and

the desert flower
in spring is most
clear and delicate

and the memory
will sustain us

and the cool
spring rains
will repudiate
our thirst

and the colors
and the light
will bless the
dark wait

"I have come
that
you might have
life
and have it
more
abundantly

do not fear
my little children
I have overcome
the darkness

the water
that
I shall give
will
turn into a
spring
inside you
welling
up to eternal
life"

12

Christ's
words
learned by
rote

mumbled

doubted
feared
forgotten
denied

recalled
desired
clung to

will spring

and night shall
become
day and day
night

without fear
now
because of Him
who said

"Fear not
I have overcome
darkness—
I am the Light"

13

Christ

the Truth
or
the lie

that
first step of
faith

toward truth
or
the lie

for life
or death

is a choice

we seek
in the light
of Christ

Winter Weather

(A Letter to a Young Artist)

1

Somewhere under
all that snow

green threads
in
seeds
are coiling
for a spring

Billie

and more than
the Milky Way
and all the
stars at night

will be flowers
in the Rockies
and the Alps

(even in tundra
zones
I have seen
them
blooming in snow)

God is love

2

You are in Denver
and
I in Boston Now

drinking coffee
at Brighams

I just saw
a
wrinkled man
with
his son carrying
a
big Christmas
present

I hit my tooth
with
the coffee cup
pretending
not to notice

I walk into doors
and
run into parking
meters
remembering him

for a second I saw

3

Who or what
could
take anything
or
anyone away

distance can't
sleep can't

I'm wondering
what
will death be

4

So don't be
afraid Billie

in every city
sanctuary lamps
burn—many

do not know
what they are
for

or that they
are burning

spending themselves
witnessing

they can do
no
more—for that
they
were made

a costly waste?

5

Magdalen's perfume
pots

did she laugh
letting
the nard flow

I am sure
she
did and that

only Christ
knew
and herself

laughing with
Him

6

No matter
what
you do son

brother sister
father mother

child—nothing
will matter

but burning
slowly
steadily evenly
alone
suspended
near
the altar

this is all
I know
or am sure of

7

Maybe

when we have
passed
our souls will
fly
as tongues of
fire
into His fire

this is beyond
my imaging

somehow
to have burned
here

is enough for me

8

I hope I hear
your
voice again

Billie

be like God
laughing
embracing all
keeping
no one—nothing

Credo

The talent to be an artist
   as all other talents
is not given to the individual
   to keep, but to share

and every talent shared
   benefits both the individual
and the community—

and every thing that benefits
   an individual and the community

benefits the whole human family
   in ways as countless as grains
of sand, as immeasurable as the
   swell of the sea—

and the call to be an artist
   is a call to act publicly
and what call can be more sacred
   than to serve the human family?

so the process begins
   the learning of the craft
from the first spontaneous crayon
   mark on a blank page
with all the surprise of making
   something new—with all the
excitement of seeing pure color
   to the mature painting with its
delicate shades, blending, and tints
   (for nature shows no pure colors)
the artist says "look" and
   becomes the child again—

the woman with child, her heaviness
her hope, her patience
(for birth cannot be forced)
the new life
is a slow unfolding of a plan
a mysterious plan which is
believed in, not understood
for the fashioning occurs within
growth is a matter of blood and bone
—hidden—

and the word is made flesh
always a particular birth
growth, suffering, death
resurrection, ascension—for new life
the infinite in the finite
spirit in flesh

the infinite is down in the
darkest, profoundest vault
of our being—in the forgotten
well-house, the deep cistern

and its silence is redemption—is grace—

and the stage is an altar
the roots of drama lie in liturgy
in ancient Greece, in religious festivals
and celebrations
in Europe, in the Easter liturgy with its
quem quaeritis trope
in the Far East, in the temple dances
the shadow puppets, and the *No* theatre
where gods entertain men
and men entertain gods—

and the call of the artist
is the call to faith
to find light in darkness
to believe that we can have new life

that we can give new life
   that daily dyings mean daily rebirths
into a strange new world
   blessed with color and light—
and the call to the artist
   is the call to affirm that
old truth of Genesis
   so simple, that indeed
He created all things
   He created all things good

and the truth of the Evangelist
   it is good to be here—
   He came that we may have new
   life and have it abundantly—
   He came to make all things new

and the artist may come to realize
   that he partakes of a paradox—
   that what he has created
   had nothing to do with him
   yet everything to do with him
that through some inclination
   he says 'yes' and brings to birth
what was not, but now is

his task—to join the psalmists
   prophets, priests, and kings
to join the Christ
   in a hymn of praise to the Father
in the Spirit
   to continue the hymn without end

to join the Christ in finding God
   in the leper, the prostitute
   the homosexual
   the lesbian
—all outcasts of man
   for if Christ did anything
He affirmed the human—

the Divine cannot be captured
   it is given
   it is hidden
mystery lives in the heart

which some
   call sacred
one terribly wounded
   but more terribly
aware of its tremendous dignity

INDEX

ADDENDA

For copies of
IN EMBRACE,
this collection of poetry,
call Life In Christ—801-942-4151 or
FAX—801-942-2226 or write to

Life in Christ
P.O. Box 1283
Sandy, Ut 84091

For copies of
APPOINTMENTS WITH THE LITTLE KING,
THE LEGEND OF THE HOLY CHILD OF ATOCHA,
or *THE LEGEND OF ST. CHRISTOPHER*
call Quiet Vision
(toll free) 1-800-442-4018
or write

Quiet Vision
12155 Mountain Shadow Road
Sandy, UT 84092-5823

For copies of the play, *JULIAN,*
call Pioneer Drama Service
(toll free) 1-800-333-7262.

For copies of
THE LOST CHILD,
THE STORY OF OUR LADY OF GUADALUPE,
or *THE STORY OF SAINT PATRICK*
call Paulist Press
(toll free) 1-800-218-1903.